Contents:

Chapter 1:   Incredible Money-Making Hints

1 Trade other forms of advertising with people who link to your web site. You could trade e-zine ads, print ads, autoresponder ads, classified ads, e-book ads, etc. It doesn't always have to be link for link or e-zine ad for e-zine ads. Just make sure it's a fair trade for you.

2 Give away web space to people for free. Since you are giving it away for free, request they link to your site by placing your ad or banner to the site. Some day you could have hundreds or thousands of web sites advertising your web site for only the cost of your web space.

3 Join or create a web ring. A web ring is a group of web sites on a similar subject that have agreed to link together. To find a web ring to join, type the keywords "web rings" into your search engine of choice. Just think, everyone who participates in the web ring is linked to your web site.

4 Create an online club or association. Tell your visitors what's included in the membership and what it costs to join. Offer them a free membership if, in exchange, they link to your web site. Just think, you will either make money or get some no-cost advertising

5 Allow people to use an online service or some utilities from your web site if, in exchange, they link to your web site. The online service could be an e-mail account, search engine submission, web page design, copywriting, proofreading, etc. If they don't want to link, you could offer them a subscription fee for the service.

6 Offer a free e-book to your web site visitors. The e-book should

be related to your target audience. Allow them to give the e-book to their own web site visitors by linking directly to your web site. You could also allow them to upload the e-book to their own web site and give it away. Just include your link in it.

7 You could offer your visitors a discount on all the products you sell if they subscribe to your free e-zine. For example, you could say, "Subscribe to our free e-zine and get 50% off all our products!" Another example, "Subscribe to our free e-zine and get $8 off our brand new e-book!"

8 You could offer your visitors a free e-book if they subscribe to your free e-zine. For example, you could say, "Subscribe to our free e-zine and get our new e-book for free!" Another example, "Subscribe to our free e-zine and get five e-books with full give-away rights!"

9 You could offer your visitors a free subscription to your private web site if they subscribe to your free e-zine. For example, you could say, "Subscribe to our free e-zine and get free access to our private membership web site!" Another example, "Subscribe to our free e-zine and get a 3-month trial membership to our Members Only web site!"

10 You could offer your visitors a free advertisement in your free e-zine if they subscribe. For example, you could say, "Subscribe to our free e-zine and get a no-cost e-zine ad! Another example, "Subscribe to our free e-zine and get a free classified ad!"

11 You could offer your visitors a free, tangible gift if they subscribe to your free e-zine. For example, you could say, "Subscribe to our free e-zine and get our new report by mail!" Another example, "Subscribe to our free e-zine and get our new tips

booklet by mail!"

12 You could offer free automatic entry into your contest or sweepstake if they subscribe to your free e-zine. For example, you could say, "Subscribe to our free e-zine and get free, automatic entry into our contest!" Another example, "Subscribe to our free e-zine for a chance to win a huge advertising package

13 You could tell your visitors that you offer original content in your free e-zine. For example, you could say, "Subscribe to our free e-zine and get our all-original content!" Another example, "Subscribe to our free e-zine and get the latest, up-to-date business news!"

14 You could tell your visitors to read a sample issue of your free e-zine on your web site. For example, you could say, "Read a sample issue before you subscribe to our free e-zine!" Another example, "Check out a sample article before you decide to subscribe to our free e-zine!"

15 You could offer your visitors free software if they subscribe to your free e-zine. For example, you could say, "Subscribe to our free e-zine and get our new marketing software free!" Another example, "Subscribe to our free e-zine and download our e-book software for free!"

16 You could offer your visitors a free sign up to your affiliate program if they subscribe to your free e-zine. For example, you could say, "Subscribe to our free e-zine and gain access to our profitable affiliate program!" Another example, "Get a free subscription to our affiliate training newsletter when you become one of our affiliates!"

17 You could offer your visitors a free web service, like free e-mail, if they subscribe to your free e-zine. For example, you could say, "Subscribe to our free e-zine and get a free bonus e-mail account!" Another example, "Subscribe to our free e-zine and get a free autoresponder!"

18 You could publish some of your current e-zine subscribers' testimonials on your web site. For example, you could say, "Why put off subscribing? Just see what other subscribers are saying!" Another example, "Subscribe today and experience the benefits the people below are experiencing!"

19 You could publish any positive reviews you have received about your free e-zine on your web site. For example, you could say, "Just read this review from (publication name) about our free e-zine!" Another example, "Check out our e-zine review in (magazine name)!"

20 You could tell your visitors what's going to be published in your next e-zine issue. For example, you could say, "Subscribe now so you don't miss our next issue about (topic)!" Another example, "Subscribe today and learn about how to (topic) in next week's issue 21 You could tell your visitors that they have the right to republish your e-zine's content on their own web site if they subscribe to your free e-zine. For example, you could say, "Subscribe to our free e-zine and we will give you the right to republish our content on your website or in your e-zine!"

22 You could publish a list of well-known, famous, or respected people who have subscribed to your free e-zine. For example, you could say, "Just look at who else is subscribed!" Another example, "Look at all the experts who have subscribed to our e-zine!"

23 You could tell your visitors what a subscription to your free e-zine is worth in dollars. For example, you could say, "Subscribe to our free e-zine. We used to charge $120 a year for a subscription." Another example, "Subscribe to our free e-zine! (Valued at $99!)"

24 You could tell your visitors all the major benefits of subscribing to your e-zine. For example, you could say, "Just look at all the benefits you'll received when you subscribe to our free e-zine!" Another example, "Subscribe to our free e-zine and get all these benefits!

25 You could tell your visitors how many people have already subscribed to your e-zine. For example, you could say, "Subscribe to our free e-zine! 14,897 subscribers can't be wrong!" Another example, "Subscribe to our free e-zine! 13,976 have already subscribed!

26 You could tell your visitors that a subscription to your free e-zine is only available for a limited time. For example, you could say, "Subscribe to our free e-zine before we start to charge for this original content!" Another example, "Subscribe to our free e-zine and your subscription will stay free even, if down the road, we decide to charge a subscription fee!"

27 People love to get free things. A free e-book is perfect. They will visit your web site to get the free valuable information. You could also start your own free e-book directory and allow other authors to submit their e-books. You could be offering hundreds of free e-books in no time!

28 Give away the full version of your e-book in exchange for testimonials. You can use these customer statements to improve

your ad's effectiveness. It would work for free or paid e-books! You could offer sample excerpts or chapters to give them a taste of it.

29 When you write and give away a free e-book you will become known as an expert. This will enable you to gain people's trust and they will buy your main product or service quicker. You may get offers from other people wanting you to speak, consult, coach, etc.

30 You could have a famous and respectable person on your banner ad representing your product, web site or service. People will click because they'll trust them over you. For example you could say, "See what (name) says about our software!"

Chapter 2:   Laser-Guided Web Marketing Campaigns

1 Use a handwritten letter on your ad copy instead of text. Write the ad on a piece of paper, scan it and publish the ad on your web page. Adding a personal touch will always increase your sales. If you don't want to write the whole letter by hand, you could just put your signature at the end.

2 Publish a list of famous and respected customers who have bought from you on your ad copy. People will think that if these people bought from you, they should also trust your business and purchase your products. Make sure to get their permission first.
For example, you could say, "Here is a list of some of our most valued customers…"

3 Show 'before' and 'after' photos for your products on your web

page copy. Show the problem picture and then beside it, show the picture of how the problem was resolved when they used your product. This will give your prospects a clearer mental image of the possible benefits of using your product.

4 Include an article or review which has been written about you or your business with your ad copy. This will show people that your business is respected and will increase your credibility. You could include the full review, an excerpt of it or link to the reviewer's web site.

5 When you offer free bonuses in your ad copy, also list the dollar value beside each bonus. People will feel they're getting a good deal and it will increase the value of your product. For example, you could say "Bonus 1# Free Internet Advertising E-book valued at $47!"

6 Hire a famous person to endorse your product or service. Make sure the person is well-known to your target audience. Include their picture and statements in your ad copy. Using a picture endorsement is more powerful because it shows the endorser likes your product enough to show his or her face.

7 Include your own picture in your ad copy. This will show people that you're not hiding behind your ad copy and will increase their trust. Also, include your contact information below the picture and a brief statement or quote. If you feel adventurous, you could include an online audio sound bite or video clip of yourself.

8 Tell your potential customers in your ad copy that you will donate a percentage of their purchase price to a specific charity. This will show them you really care about people. They may just buy your

product so their money will go to the charity. For example, you could say, "I will donate .75 cents from each order to the (name) Foundation."

9 Ask your potential customers plenty of 'yes' and 'no' questions in your ad copy. The questions should remind them of their problem and make them think about what will happen if they don't purchase your product. For example, you could say, "Do you want to get out of debt?" "Do you want to have financial security?"

10 Tell your potential customers they will receive a free prize if they find the five words in your ad copy that are misspelled or spelled backwards. The longer you can keep someone reading your copy, the greater chance of them purchasing. You could also have them find hidden links, hidden graphics, etc.

11 Give your prospects extra incentives so they will order quicker. It could be free shipping, a faster shipping option, free gift-wrapping, etc. For example, you could say, "Free gift-wrapping to the first 1000 people who order." Another example, "Free shipping to anyone who orders before (date)."

12 Make your small business look big on the world wide web. Design your web site using professional graphics, ordering systems, organized layouts, etc. For example, on the web no one really knows if you're a one-man business or huge corporation, unless you tell them. Just design your web site to look professional.

13 Attract a lot more customers by giving them clear ordering instructions. Give them all the information they need so they can complete their order easily. For example, you could say, "Please fill out all of the order form below. We accept all major credit cards and online checks. Please click the "Order" button only once. You don't

want to get double charged."

14 Give your customers buying incentives so they'll make repeat purchases. Offer them discounts, free gifts, bonus points, etc. For example, if you give your customers points every time they buy something, they will start collecting them and buy more things. They will want to save up enough points to get a free product.

15 Tell people about your site whenever you get a chance. Those people will tell other people and so on. It's a cheap way to multiply your advertising. For example, if you're at a grocery store, mention it to people you talk to; the check clerk, the bag boy, etc. Every little bit helps.

16 Write and send press releases for your web site. Use strong headlines, make it newsworthy, and tell the journalist why their readers would like it. You could increase your chances of getting your release read or published by communicating with editors regularly and creating a professional friendship with them.

17 Use a lot of headlines on your web site and e-zine. Some types of headlines are free offers, questions, problem solvers, sales, and statistics. For example, "Free E-book", "Want To Get Out Of Debt?", "Free Article", etc. You could also turn the headlines into graphics to make them look more professional.

18 Design graphics, templates, buttons and banner ads for other sites. Allow people to use them in exchange for your web link on their home page. For example, you could require the users to say on their web site, "These graphics were made possible by (your business name and web site address)."

19 Use time-saving promotional software. You can automate your search engine submissions, posting to online classified sites, etc. You may have to buy them, but you'll make up the money you spend by getting your other business requirements completed faster. Sometimes you can find this type of software for free on the web.

20 Advertise your online business by dressing in clothes that are imprinted with your ads. It could be a T-shirt, ball cap, coat, etc. You would want to especially do this if you are going to a crowded event, like a football game, a county fair, party, dance, a social club, etc.

21 Trade links with other web sites. They should be related to the subject of your web site. Instead of trading links, you could also trade banner ads, half page ads, classified ads, etc. If they turn down your trade offer, you could offer them some extra in-centives like free things and extra free ad space.

22 Start an e-zine for your web site. When people read each issue they'll be reminded to revisit your web site. They'll see your product ad more than just once, which will increase your orders. You'll need to have at least 50% original content in it so people don't unsubscribe because they read your information in other e-zines.

23 Form an online community. It could be an online message board, e-mail discussion list or chat room. When people get involved in your community, they will regularly return to communicate with others. You could also invite your online community to free "how to" classes hosted in your chat room or by teleconference.

24 Write articles and submit them to e-zines, web sites and magazines that accept article submissions. Include your business information and web address at the end of the article. You could also give the editors extra incentives to publish your article, like freebies, affiliate commissions, offers to publish their article, etc. 25 Give away an electronic freebie with your ad on it. Allow your visitors to give the freebie away as well. This'll increase your ad exposure and attract people to your web site at the same time. You could also use it as a bonus for another product you sell or as a free surprise gift for your most loyal customers.

26 Combine your products or services into one big package deal with offerings from other businesses. You could share a web site and advertise the pack-age deal which would mean double the traffic. It could be one or more business. If the business is your competition, you would want to use a neutral product.

27 Submit your freebie to the online directories that list your particular item or service for free. If you're offering a free e-zine, submit it to all the free e-zine directories on the Internet. There are free e-book directories, web site directories, general freebie directories, free article directories, etc.

28 Participate on message boards. Post answers to other people's questions, ask questions and post appropriate information. Include your signature file
at the end of all your postings. Some message boards let you include a text link at the end of your message. Plus you can learn great tips reading all the postings.

29 Exchange classified or sponsor ads with other free e-zine publishers. If there is a huge subscriber difference between e-zines,

one can run more ads to make up for it. You could also offer free items or affiliate commissions. Another idea would be to offer them an ad on your web site too.

30 Post your ad on free advertising areas on the Internet. You can post it on free classified ad sites, free for all links sites, newsgroups that allow ads, free yellow page directories, etc. Of course all of those areas have different rules for submissions so you may have to structure your offer differently each time.

Chapter 3: **Little-Known Net Business Advice**

1 You could offer your potential customers a bonus coupon when they buy one of your products. It could be a coupon for another product you sell. For example, you could say, "Free Bonus! A 30% Off Coupon For Our New E-book! How To..." Another example, "Free Bonus! My Good Friend (their name) Is Allowing Me To Give A Free 40% Off Coupon For His New Product (product name)!"

2 Create a memorable logo and slogan to brand your business on the Internet. When people see your slogan or logo it will remind them of your business. For example, how many times have you heard a product name and thought of their slogan? How many times have you seen a logo and it made you think of a business or product?

3 Multiply your marketing all over the Internet by creating free bonuses for other businesses' products. You just include your ad somewhere on the bonus. For example, if your target audience is network marketers, you create bonuses for MLM companies.

4 Offer to buy advertising space inside electronic products like e-books, software, subscription sites, etc. It will be cheaper than running any kind of print ads. For example, if you're selling to entrepreneurs, you would want to buy advertising space in business-related e-books, reports and subscription web sites.

5 Increase your sales by adjusting your product or service to attract other target audiences. This may mean redesigning or adding to it. For example, if you're selling an e-book about how to increase your online sales, you could rewrite parts of it so that it'd also apply to offline businesses.

6 Test the prices of your product or service. You may increase the perceived value by raising your price while a lower price may decrease your sales. One effective way to see which price to charge would be to take one of your products and auction it off at an online auction. This final bid would be close to the price you need to sell it at.

7 Use your product's features to support all of your benefits. Just because benefits are more important, don't forget to list the features. For example, you could say, "Our (product) is very easy to carry because of our durable plastic cover."

8 Market yourself or your business as an expert. Most people have been told throughout their lives to trust and respect the authoritative figures in society. For example, "Our (topic) business has the largest selection in the world!" Another example, "I've read over 200 books on Internet marketing!"

9 Train yourself and your employees to be polite to all your customers, even if they're shouting. Solve their problem quickly and it may even turn into a sale. For example, you could have posters

hanging in the workplace. Reminding staff to be polite, curious and helpful to your customers.

10 Give your visitors a good impression when they first visit your web site. Don't make a banner ad the first thing they see at the top of your home page. For example, if you visited a web site and it had a lot of banners all over it, would you stick around to read their offer?

11 Provide a privacy statement and all your contact information on every page of your web site. This'll persuade your visitors and prospects to trust you. For example, if your contact information was only on your home page and they had a question about ordering one of your products on another page, they might just get frustrated and leave your web site.

12 Publish a picture of yourself in your ads this will show people that you're not hiding behind your web site and you're not afraid to back up your product. For example, it could be a picture of you using the product you're selling. Another example, it could be a picture of you in a smart business suit.

13 List how many famous or respected people have purchased your product in your ads. These people should be fairly well-known by your target audience. For example, you could say "Just look below to see a list all the corporate clients we've helped!" Another example, "We've had many experts buy our product in the past, just take a look…"

14 Publish the results of any tests your product has passed in your ad. Your product may have passed a durability test, safety test, quality test, etc. For example, you could say, "Our product has passed all safety tests required by law." Another example, "We don't

sell any product unless it passes our rigorous durability test first."

15 Publish the results of any positive surveys you've taken from your customers in your ads. Just survey your current customers and list the results. For example, "2557 first-time customers out of 2600 surveyed say they would buy our product again!"

16 List any publications which have written about your business in your ads. It could be a product review, on a top ten list, an article, etc. For example, "(title) magazine says....," "(title) Times say....," "(title) news says...," etc. Another example, "(title) magazine rates our product 10 out of 10!"

17 List any related books that you've written in your ads. When you list a book or books you've written, it gives you credibility because it shows you're an expert. For example, you could say, "I've written over ten books and e-books on marketing and copywriting including the best seller..."

18 Have a professional looking web site to publish your ad on. When people visit your site and it looks unprofessional, they'll relate that to your product. For example, haven't you ever read an ad that made you really want to buy, but the look of the web site turned you off so much that you just walked away?

19 Publish any endorsements from famous people in your ad. Some people will think if a famous person enjoys your product, so will they. For example, you could say, "Just look at what the famous (their name) had to say!" Another example, "Here's what marketing expert (their name) had to say!

20 Use a money-back guarantee in your ad. This will remove the risk for your potential customers and show them that you stand

behind your product. For example, "If you are not completely satisfied I will give you double your money back!" Another example, "You have no risk with our lifetime money-back guarantee!

21 Provide testimonials from satisfied customers in your ads. The testimonials should include specific and believable results your customers have received. For example, you could say "(their name) from Ohio said..." Another example, "A milkman from Miami, Florida said that…"

22 Tell your prospects that you offer free delivery. This may cost you a bit of money but you will gain the extra customers to make up for it. For example, "Unlike our competition we have free delivery!" Another example, "FREE Shipping! To The First 500 Who Order!"

23 Know exactly what you want your ad copy to accomplish. It could be to qualify prospects, make sales, generate leads, attract web traffic, etc. For example, if you want to increase traffic, offer them something for free. If you want to sell a product, use benefits, limited time offers, bonuses, guarantees, etc.

24 Make a complete list of your product's benefits and features. Begin your ad with the most important benefit either in your headline or first sentence. For example, your headline could say, "Write Joint Venture Proposals In Minutes!" Another example, "Would You Like To Work At Home?"

25 Make your ad benefits as specific as possible. Include exact numbers, percentages, times, colors, smells, sounds, descriptive adjectives, etc. For example, "Five tactics for increasing your profits by over 234%!" Another example, "How to write your own e-book in 9hrs 11mins or less!"

26 List all the ways your product is different from your competitions. Include in your ad copy all the differences which make your product better than theirs. For example, you could say, "Our product comes with a 5 year warranty unlike the competition." Another example, "Our competition doesn't offer any bonuses but we offer 5 of them!"

27 Use graphics, pictures and drawings of people actually using your product to solve their problem. Include a picture that also shows the results. For example, use a picture of someone smiling while using your product. Another example, use a picture of someone who chose not to use your product, showing the problems that weren't solved.

28 Make a list of your target audience. Write down what reasons would attract them to purchase your product. Include those reasons in your ad copy. For example, if my target audience was business owners and affiliate marketers, I would write down things like - make money, increase sales, cut costs, etc.

29 Include any proven facts in your ad copy. They could be customer surveys, scientific tests, product reviews, etc. For example, you could say, "FACT: Our product withstood an elephant walking over it!" Another example, "(business name) Research found that our product reduces stress by 325%."

30 Look for different ways to prove your business and products to your audience. You could collect testimonials, hold surveys, do scientific tests, etc. For example, if you

were selling a money-making product, you could use a picture of one of your actual checks.

Chapter 4:   Secret Selling Blueprints

1 Use a "P.S." at the end of your ad copy. This is where you either want to repeat a strong benefit or use a strong close, like a free bonus. For example, "P.S. You can get (product), worth over ($), for the low price of ($)!" Another example, "P.S. I can not guarantee the (No.) bonuses will be here tomorrow!"

2 You could end your ad copy with a discounted price. Just list your regular price and then offer a discounted price off the order 'right now'. You could also offer a rebate that takes effect instantly. For example, you could say, "Instead of paying $99, you could order now and get an instant rebate of $20 - you only pay $79!"

3 You could end your ad copy with a free sample or trial of your product. If your ad didn't attract them to buy, maybe a free sample or trial would. If you were selling an e-book, you could give them a free sample at the end of your ad copy. For example, you could say, "If you're still not sure about ordering, download a FREE sample chapter!

4 Sell a few back-end products that are not related to your main product but are needed by all humans. Every customer that buys from you is human. Think about it - everyone eats, right? For example, you could say, "Free

Bonus 1# A Free $30 Dollar Coupon to the Restaurant of Your Choice!"

5 Take on as many of your business' chores as you can handle; outsource what you can't. Only you can determine how your business operates. You don't want too many people making all your decisions, but you don't want to take on so much responsibility that you become a workaholic.

6 Try out new business opportunities. You could combine them with your current business. It could add an extra profit stream to your web site. You could join affiliate programs, MLMs, drop ship selling programs, etc. Another idea would be to joint venture with other businesses.

7 Create an alliance with 3 or 4 web sites. Include each of your ads or banners on the other web sites. You will all share targeted traffic with each other. For example, you would instantly have 3 web sites selling for you without paying them an affiliate income. You would just be giving them ad space on your web site.

8 Create a free e-zine directory. You'll attract a lot of traffic from e-zine publishers and people who want to subscribe to the e-zines. Your listings could include name, subscription instructions, publisher's name, etc. Of course you could put your own e-zine listing at the top of your directory to get extra exposure.

9 When you offer a freebie from your site, submit it to

freebie sites. They provide target categories which mean targeted traffic. So if you're submitting software, you could submit it to the "free software" section. Just remember, some freebie sites want you to link to their web site before they will list your freebie submission.

10 Make your visitors curious about your product by telling them they need to sign up to get into a password protected site to read the rest of the ad. This will give your product extra perceived value because it is so well guarded. Just like a diamond in a bank vault.

11 Remember the little things about your web pages really count. Include the title of your site at the top right corner, a description about your site, etc. For example, if I visited your web site and didn't know or understand what it was all about, I would probably leave right away.

12 Start your own Internet radio station. It could be related to the theme of your web site and you could advertise your products over the station. You could also charge other businesses advertising on your station. You could start a music station or something like a talk radio station.

13 Turn your banner ad into a trivia question. Post the question on the banner and tell readers they can win a prize if they answer the question at your site. People love trivia because it makes them feel smart when they get the right answer. The prize is just an extra incentive for them to click on your banner.

14 Motivate people to buy your product. Tell them positive things. For example, you could say, "You can now reach your goals and change your life if you buy our product." If you come across positive in your ad copy, they will become positive about reaching their goals using your product.

15 Get your sales letters and web site evaluated for free. Visit business discussion boards and ask other participants to evaluate them. Don't get discouraged if someone gives you a lot of negative feedback about your web site. Most people are only trying to help you. Take the criticism constructively.

16 Get your products or services evaluated for free. You can give your product for free in exchange for evaluations and even testimonials. You will find out any problems with your product before you sell it. You might also discover new uses or selling points for your product too.

17 Keep your loyal customers happy because they are your future profits. Give them discounts and free gifts as often as possible. If you are thoughtful and loyal to your customers, most of them will be your customers forever. They will make up about 80% of your business and profits.

18 Clone your advertisements all over the Internet by allowing your visitors to give your online freebies away. Just include your ad somewhere inside them. You could also start an affiliate program and pay people commissions to run your ads. You could also give your affiliates viral

marketing tools to use like e-books or articles.

19 Make it easy for your affiliates to make sales. Give them proven ads to use, make it easy for prospects to order and provide helpful affiliate statistics. Affiliates want high or fair commissions, notification of sales, lifetime income, and residual income, a good tracking system and professional training.

20 Persuade e-zine publishers or webmasters to run your ad for free. Just allow them to join your affiliate program and earn commission on the sales. You could also offer them a freebie, such as the product you're selling for free, an advertisement in your e-zine in return, etc. It also helps to compliment the publishers as well as praising their e-zines.

21 Make your products sell quickly by adding a lot of bonuses. You could get the free bonuses for little or no cost by joint venturing with other businesses. You could go to the "freebies" directories and find things. Then you could ask the legal owner's permission to use the item as a free bonus for your product.

22 Test different web site color themes to see which combination will sell your product better. You can also test the size and style of your web site text. For example, red usually signals: stop, anger, excitement, love, sex, fun, etc. Another example, blue usually signals: relaxation, authority, coolness, etc.

23 Promise your readers an end result or outcome in your ad. You must give them a solid guarantee that your product will solve their problem. For example, you could say, "I personally guarantee you will get over your shyness in 10 days or less or your money back."

24 Never assume people believe the information in your ad copy. You need to back-up all your claims with indisputable evidence. For example, you could include testimonials, expert endorsements, third party tests or studies, strong guarantees, a list of customers, pictures of customers, etc.

25 Give your customers free shipping. If you can't afford that, you can give free shipping to customers who buy over a certain dollar amount to raise profits. You could also charge other businesses for inserting ads in your product package. This will make up for your free shipping losses.

26 Test your web site regularly for ordering glitches, bad links, broken graphics, etc. Those types of errors will make your business look unprofessional. If your visitors can't order, navigate to where they want to go or see pictures of your product, they likely won't revisit or order.

27 Use free advertising as much as possible. Test a wide variety of free advertising options like banner and link exchanges, classifieds, newsgroups, ad swaps, joint venturing, viral marketing, web rings, message boards, trading content, etc. Don't be afraid to try something new.

28 Build credibility for your business by publishing an e-

zine and writing articles. Your customers and prospects will see you as an expert and trust you. You could also submit your articles to other e-zines for republishing and publicity. Just require them to include your resource box at the end of the article.

29 Answer all your e-mail messages as quickly as possible. Nothing will lose a sale quicker than not responding to a prospect in time. If you don't, it could anger your customers and they could ask for a refund. You may lose a sale because they want you to answer a question before they order.

30 Build a professional looking web site even if you have a small budget. You could use free graphics, designs, list servers and other tools offered online. Just go to your search engine or web directory of choice and type in "free (what you want)" and you will usually find it.

Chapter 5   Phenomenal Online Sales Formulas

1 Start publishing an extra issue of your e-zine every week. You could charge a recurring monthly subscription for the free subscribers who want to view the extra issue(s) each week. You could also include no ads in the extra issue because you're charging a subscription fee.

2 Don't load your web site with a lot of high tech clutter. Your visitors may miss your whole sales message. Haven't you ever visited a web site which had graphic ads, text scrolling and flashing words all crammed together? If you

have, it was likely you found it confusing and hard on the eyes and you just said 'forget it'.

3 Don't use unnecessary words or phrases on your site. You only have so much time to get your visitor's attention and interest; make every word count. Use short words, phrases, sentences and paragraphs. Also highlight attention-grabbing words like love, money, sex, etc.

4 Don't make the mistake and think that everyone will totally understand your web site message. Use descriptive words and examples to get your point across more smoothly. Don't use hard to understand words that they might have to look up in a dictionary because they won't, they'll just leave your web site.

5 Don't write your strongest point or benefit only once. You should repeat it at least 3 times because some people may miss it. Also when you repeat something it gets stored in your prospect's brain easier. This may persuade them to buy later on down the road because they will remember it when they really need or want your products

6 Don't push all your words together on your web site. People like to skim; use plenty of headings and sub-headings. People don't have time to search and read through every word. It's also harder to read online than offline. But you could remind them they could print out your web page to read it later when they are offline.

7 Don't use site content your target audience isn't interested in. If people are coming to your site to find information about fishing, don't include soccer content.

That rule also applies to your free e-zine, your free e-book, the products you sell, the affiliate programs you promote, etc.

8 Don't use 50 different content formats all over your web site. Try to use only one or two of the same fonts, text sizes, text colors, etc. You don't want your visitors getting frustrated because they have to keep refocusing their eyes. Plus it looks unprofessional not to have a consistent look throughout your web site.

9 Offer easy navigation. People will leave quicker if they have a hard time finding what they're looking for. Don't get them lost or they will leave. You could have a keyword search box, a side, top or bottom navigation bar, a web site map, etc.

10 Don't let selling words and phrases go unnoticed. Highlight important words and phrases with color, bolding, italics, underlining, etc. Also think about about each and every word you use on your web site. Ask yourself "Is this word going to persuade them to buy my product, join my affiliate program, subscribe to my e-zine", etc.

11 Form a strategic alliance with other related but non-competing businesses. You'll be able to beat your competition by selling to a larger audience, sharing advertising costs, trading business strategies, bartering both goods and services, gaining new products to sell, packaging products together, etc.

12 Address your targeted audience on your business site.

For example, "Welcome Internet Marketers". If you have more than one, address them all. When you want to get their attention in the ad copy, you could say, "Attention! All Internet marketers, business owners, opportunity seekers and other entrepreneurs."

13 Make sure your content and graphics are relevant to your web site's theme. You wouldn't want to use a bird graphic on a business web site, unless the bird had a business suit on or was doing something business related. That would grab your prospects' attention and the bird would convey the impression that you sell to businesses or that you are a business.

14 Alert visitors by e-mail when you add new content to your web site. This will remind people to revisit your web site. For example, you could say on your web site, "Sign up to our opt-in list to be reminded in the future when our web site is updated or we add new products."

15 Offer a way for visitors to contact you on each web page. List your e-mail address, fax number and phone number. If you're selling a product, remind them to order on each page. If you're giving away a free subscription to your e-zine, remind them to subscribe on every page.

16 Give people the option of viewing your web site offline. Offer it by way of an autoresponder message or by a printer-friendly web page. They may forward it to their friends or family members if it's an e-mail or they may give it to them if they have it printed out.

17 Make sure that at least 50% of your content is original. The other option is to offer something else original other

than content, like software or an online utility. You need to offer something they can't go anywhere else to get. Then they can't think, "Well I saw another web site that has that same free e-book so I'll just go there instead."

18 Offer your visitors incentives for revisiting your web site. You could give them new content, e-books, software, e-zines, etc. Offer a new weekly contest so they have to revisit every week to re-enter. Offer a new, original freebie every week so they have to revisit. You can just ask them to sign up to a reminder e-mail list.

19 Publish FAQs for your business, products and web site. They could have questions about multiple parts of your business. You could answer questions about your products, business, web site, free e-zine, affiliate program, message board, chat room, free e-book and other services.

20 Make sure all links on the navigational bar are clickable. If people can't get to where they want to go, they will leave. It's a good idea to go through your whole web site and check all your links once
in awhile. There are also software programs that can do it for you too.

21 Organize your web site in a logical and profitable sequence. You don't want to give away a freebie before they learn about the product(s) you're selling. Make your visitors see at least one or two of your ads before they get to your freebie. Then include those ads somewhere in or around your freebie.

22 Use plenty of examples in your ad copy. This will allow

your whole target audience to understand your sales pitch completely. If they don't understand your product offer, how do you expect them to buy? Have a few younger kids read it. If they understand it, you'll know an older person will definitely understand it.

23 Gain extra credibility by using terms your readers may not understand but can follow, by explaining them in simple terms. This will show you're an expert. People often find it interesting to see new words as they could get bored seeing the same old words every day.

24 Reveal how excited you are about the product. You could use words, or even a picture of yourself looking very excited. For example, you could say in your ad copy, "I'm super EXCITED about our new product!" Another example, "I'm so PUMPED UP about our new product I can't wait to tell you about it!"

25 Tell your target audience you were in their current position. Next, tell them how your product pulled you out of that position. For example, you could say in your ad copy, "Don't worry, I used to be just like you. I was way over my head in debt. But I decided to create a financial formula so no one else would ever go through all the pain and humiliation of bankruptcy like I did."

26 Challenge your readers at the end of your ad. Make a bet with them; if your product doesn't solve their problem, offer them a free product in return. People love to gamble and most are greedy. You're just using it to your advantage so you can sell them your product or service. Some people

like to gamble just because it's fun.

27 Get your audience involved in your ad by asking them questions. They'll automatically want to answer the questions in their mind. For example, you could say in your ad copy, "Where do you want to be weight-wise in the next 5 months?" Another example, "Do you want to weigh that much or more 2 years from now?"

28 Introduce yourself in your ad copy. Haven't you ever read ad copy and wondered who was selling the product halfway through? It's a big turn-off. For example, you could say, "Hello my name is (your name and a little about yourself)." Another example, "It's (your name) here, I'm going to tell you about..."

29 Start your ad with a story. It draws people right into your ad and they forget they're being sold to. For example, you could start your ad, "Once upon a time ..." Another example would be, "Last year, one of my friends and I were..."

30 Use less than seven points in your ad copy. If you start revealing too many topics, your readers might get confused and quit reading. Your points could be your benefits, guarantees, testimonials, closing, opening, postscripts, and headline. Some other points would be features, case studies, customer lists, etc.

Chapter 6:   **Revolutionary Income Concepts**

1 Gain an advantage over your competition. You should find one benefit your competition doesn't offer and use it as your main selling point. For example, if your competition doesn't offer free shipping, you should find a way to afford to offer free shipping. One way would be to charge other businesses for inserting ads in your product package.

2 Design your e-zine so it creates multiple free advertising streams. Ask readers to forward it to people they know, offer ad trades, etc. For example, you could say, "Forward this e-zine to your friends or family." Another example, "We accept ad trades from other e-zines."

3 Allow your visitors to subscribe to an update e-zine. Anytime you make changes to your web site they can receive an informative e-mail. For example, you could say, "Sign up to be reminded by e-mail when this web site is updated in the future." You could also subtly mention a product you are currently selling.

4 Focus your articles on information the targeted readers and e-zine publishers want. They will get published more often, which means free publicity. For example, if they are business e-zines, you want to write articles about starting a business, marketing, advertising, cutting costs, joint ventures, etc.

5 Use problems to attract online traffic. Find a common online problem and use your web site to solve it. People

will visit and see your ads. For example, you could say, "How To Accept Credit Cards Without Forking Over Money For A Merchant Account." Another example, "How To Get To The Top Of The Search Engines Without Being Listed."

6 Have an informative FAQ page at your web site. Anticipate questions your prospects or visitors may have; this will help improve your sales ratio. For example, "Read our Frequently Asked Questions first. It may answer your question and save you waiting for one." Another example, "Check Out Our FAQ Page If You Have Any Questions."

7 Improve your negotiation skills. This'll improve your business because you're always negotiating ad swaps, supply prices, joint ventures, wages, etc. For example, if you wanted to trade ads with an e-zine that had double the subscribers you do, they may not trade but if you offered the e-zine owner an extra ad, they might.

8 Beat your competition by giving away a similar product or service that they charge for. It could be add-on products, warranties, servicing, etc. For example, you could say, "Unlike our competition we don't charge extra for batteries." Another example, "Our competition charges up to ($) a year for soft-ware upgrades, we charge $0!"

9 Build a larger online community by giving your visitors bonuses for participating on your message boards or chat rooms. Try free products, ads, etc. For example, you could say, "Participate in our online message board and get the FREE report! How To..." Another example, "Get this free

e-book for just chatting in our chat room!"

10 Instead of starting an affiliate program, start a referral program. Give people discounts and free products for referring people to your site. For example, you could say, "Get a free e-book software for referring just 3 people to our web site." Another example, "Refer just 2 people to our web site to get a 20% discount on our new e-book!"

11 Offer free original content. It's important to give your visitors information they can't find anywhere else. If you're the only source, they'll visit your site. For example, if you write business e-books you know they are many of them out there, but if you added an unrelated topic with the business content, like science, it would be more original.

12 Give people free software. Most people like to find good deals on software for their computers. If the software is free, that is even better. For example, you could say, "FREE Accounting Software!" You could also use the software for viral marketing. Just place your ad in the software and allow people to give it away.

13 Hold free contests or sweepstakes. Most people like to win things. If you can fulfill that need, people will stop by to visit. You can also capture people's e-mail addresses. For example, "Sign up for our contest for a chance to win a new computer! You will be notified via e-mail."

14 Provide a free web directory. Create a directory of web sites on a popular topic that will attract your target audience. For example, if you had a free e-book directory

you could advertise your web site by saying something like "Get 1000 FREE E-books When You Visit (your web site address)."

15 Offer a free e-zine. Most people love to get free information that's e-mailed to them regularly. This saves them time and money. For example, you could say, "Sign up to my e-zine and learn about (topic) every week for absolutely free!" Another example, "Free Weekly Business E-zine - Save time and money learning (topic)!"

16 Make your web site look professional. You want to have your own domain name, easy navigation, attractive graphics, etc. For example, wouldn't it make you think twice about buying from a free domain name web site? Another example, if you get confused or lost at a web site, don't you immediately click out of it?

17 Let people read your ad before they get to your freebie. When you use free things to lure people to your web site, list them below your ad copy. For example, haven't you ever downloaded a free e-book and read it right away without looking at the rest of the web site?

18 Attract the target audience who would buy your product or service. A simple way to do this is to survey your existing customers. Another idea would be to address them with their group name. For example, "Dear Web Marketers..." , "Attention All Gardeners - Listen Up!", etc.

19 Test and improve your ad copy. There are many people who write an ad and never change it. Make sure you get the highest possible response rate. For example, run the ad you have ready and see how many orders you get in a week or month. After that change the headline or closing and see how many
orders you receive. Continue tweaking your ad till you get the highest amount of orders per visitors or viewers.

20 Give people urgency so they buy 'now'. Many people could be interested in your product but they'll put off buying it until later and eventually forget about it. For example, "Order Before Aug 15, 2002, and get 2 Bonuses Valued at ($)!" Another example, "Order Now! Only 1000 Members Will Be Accepted."

21 When you ship people the first product they bought, insert a flyer or brochure for your back-end product in the package. For example, if you're selling a book about gardening, you could slip in a flyer about a packet of seeds you're currently selling into the box you are shipping.

22 Give customers a free subscription to a Customers Only e-zine when they buy your product. You could include your ad for your back-end product in each issue. For example, you could say, "When you order, you will get a free subscription to our e-zine about e-books." The customers will also see your ads every week and that will increase their tendency to buy again from you. Plus a free e-zine is a good bonus to lure them to order.

23 Send your customers greeting cards on holidays or on their birthday. Include a small advertisement inside the card for your back-end product. For example, the card could say "Happy Halloween! To celebrate this holiday we are offering you 30% off our new book titled..." Another example, "Happy Birthday! For a gift we are giving a free sample of our new book titled…If you like it, you can get the full version for only ($)."

24 Tell your prospects that your product is easy to use. People don't want to buy a product that they have to read a 100 page instruction manual. For example, "Our software is user-friendly, it takes you step-by-step." Another example, "You'll get a simple 3 step instruction manual that walks you through the whole scanner set-up."

25 Send customers a free surprise gift after they order your first product. You could attach another ad with the free gift for your back-end product. For example, "Unadvertised Surprise Bonus! A free copywriting e-book!" Then inside the e-book have subtle ads for the product(s) you're selling. Above or below each page. You could also mention them within your content.

26 If you're selling an electronic product, like an e-book or report, include your ad for your back-end product somewhere inside the electronic product. For example, on the last page, title page, index, table of contents, glossary, etc. If you liked the product, wouldn't you buy again from that company?

27 Tell your prospects how long you've been in business for. People think if you've been in business for a while, you have more credibility. For example, "We've been in business for (no.) years!" Another example, "We've been serving businesses since 1935!"

28 Contact your customers by phone and ask them if they were happy with their purchase. You could tell them about your back-end product. For example, "I'm calling to thank you for purchasing our (product). I wanted to make sure you were happy with it and tell you about our new (your back-end product)..."

29 Tell your prospects your product is compact or light. People may want to take the product on a trip or don't have much room where they live. For example, "Our (product) only weighs (no.) ounces!" Another example, "Our (product) fits inside your pants' pocket!"

30 Ask your customers if they want to be updated in the future when you have new product offers. You could have them sign up to receive e-mail or snail mail updates. If they sign up this usually means they really like and trust your business because they know ahead of time all they will be getting are product offers. These people will be the easiest to sell to.

To your success,
Johnny